Failurenaire

Side Hustle Series: Affiliate Marketing

By:
The Failurenaire
(Check Out Failurenaire.com)

Table of Contents:

Table of Contents: _____ 2
Introduction: Meet the Failurenaire _____ 3
Chapter 1: What is Affiliate Marketing? _____ 7
Chapter 2: The Magic of Affiliate Marketing _____ 14
Chapter 3: Finding Your Passion _____ 20
Chapter 4: The Hunt for the Right Affiliate Programs 27
Chapter 5: Building Your Platform _____ 35
Chapter 6: Content is King _____ 42
Chapter 7: Building Your Brand _____ 49
Chapter 8: The SEO Game _____ 55
Chapter 9: Social Media Savvy _____ 61
Chapter 10: The Power of Email Marketing _____ 68
Chapter 11: Transparency and Trust _____ 75
Chapter 12: Analyzing and Optimizing _____ 81
Chapter 13: Scaling Up _____ 89
Chapter 14: Overcoming Challenges _____ 97
Chapter 15: Real Stories _____ 103
Chapter 16: Your Affiliate Marketing Tool Box ____ 108
Chapter 17: The Future of Affiliate Marketing ____ 114
Chapter 18: Why I Struggled to Successful w/ Affiliate Marketing _____ 123
Chapter 19: Your Journey…Begins Now _____ 132

Introduction: Meet the Failurenaire

Greetings, dear reader. Welcome to my Affiliate Marketing book, where I embark on the journey of introducing myself to you. My name? I go by the name of the Failurenaire. Yes, you heard it right, the Failurenaire. It's not a title I earned through grand achievements or remarkable successes. Instead, it's a badge I wear proudly, forged through the trials and tribulations of a life filled with failures.

I hail from parts unknown, a mysterious origin shrouded in ambiguity. But one thing is for certain – wherever I go, failure seems to follow. I'm notorious, not for my triumphs or victories, but for my unrelenting string of failures. It's almost comical, really. Whether it's attempting side hustles, navigating the complexities of relationships, battling with

Introduction: Meet the Failurenaire

dieting and exercise, dabbling in investing, or even predicting the outcomes of sports games, failure seems to be my constant companion.

Now, you might be wondering, why on earth would anyone want to read a book by someone who admits to being a failure? Fair question. The truth is, despite my track record of setbacks and shortcomings, I continue to strive for excellence. Call it foolish optimism or sheer stubbornness, but I refuse to let my failures define me. Instead, I choose to see them as valuable lessons – stepping stones on the path to self-improvement and personal growth.

I am by no means a guru or an expert in anything. In fact, far from it. But what I lack in expertise, I make up for in curiosity and a thirst for knowledge. I pride myself on being a Jack of all trades, master of none. I've

Introduction: Meet the Failurenaire

dabbled in a myriad of subjects, from philosophy to physics, psychology to finance. I may not be an expert in any one field, but I possess a wealth of eclectic knowledge gathered from my diverse experiences and relentless pursuit of learning.

So, why am I writing this book, you ask? It's simple – I want to share everything I've learned along the way. Every misstep, every wrong turn, every stumble – I want to lay it all bare for you, dear reader. My goal is not to impart wisdom from the pedestal of success, but rather to offer insights from the trenches of failure. I want to show you what held me back, so that you can avoid making the same mistakes. I want to empower you to do better than me, to achieve greater heights than I ever could.

Introduction: Meet the Failurenaire

In the chapters that follow, I'll be sharing my knowledge, my experiences, and yes, even my failures, with the hope that you'll find something of value in them. Please make sure you pay attention to the "Failurenaire Insights" at the end of each chapter. Whether you're a seasoned affiliate marketer professional or a budding entrepreneur, whether you're seeking inspiration or practical advice, I invite you to join me on this journey. Together, let's turn failure into fuel for success. After all, as the Failurenaire, it's what I do best.

*Disclaimer: All content in this book could lead you to making lots of money…however, this book should be treated as "Entertainment" and nothing learned from this book is guaranteed to work and make you money.

Chapter 1: What is Affiliate Marketing?

Chapter 1:

What is Affiliate Marketing?

Affiliate marketing is a game-changer in the digital age, opening up avenues for income that were unimaginable a few decades ago. But what exactly is it, and how can you harness its power? Imagine a world where you recommend products you genuinely love and get paid for it. That's the essence of affiliate marketing. It's not just about making a sale; it's about building a bridge between customers and products, creating a win-win situation for everyone involved.

At its core, affiliate marketing is about partnerships. Companies, eager to expand their reach and boost sales, team up with individuals or other businesses—affiliates—who promote their products. When a sale is made through an affiliate's recommendation, the affiliate

Chapter 1: What is Affiliate Marketing?

earns a commission. It's a simple yet powerful concept: leverage the influence of many to reach potential customers in places traditional advertising might miss.

Understanding the mechanics of affiliate marketing starts with the players involved. First, you have the merchant or retailer. This could be a giant like Amazon, a niche boutique, or even a digital product creator. They're the ones who have products to sell and are looking for ways to get those products in front of more eyes.

Then there's the affiliate, which could be you. As an affiliate, your job is to promote the merchant's products. But it's not about bombarding people with ads. Successful affiliates are storytellers, educators, and problem solvers. They understand their audience's needs and provide valuable content that integrates product recommendations naturally.

Chapter 1: What is Affiliate Marketing?

Finally, there's the consumer—the person who buys the product. They're often looking for solutions to their problems, answers to their questions, or simply recommendations on the best products to buy. When they make a purchase through an affiliate's link, everyone wins: the merchant makes a sale, the affiliate earns a commission, and the consumer finds what they were looking for.

To get started with affiliate marketing, it's crucial to understand the platforms that facilitate these partnerships. Affiliate networks like Amazon Associates, ClickBank, and Commission Junction act as intermediaries, connecting merchants with affiliates. These networks provide the infrastructure needed to track sales, manage payments, and offer a variety of products to promote.

Chapter 1: What is Affiliate Marketing?

Choosing the right products to promote is an art in itself. It's not just about picking high-commission items; it's about aligning those products with your audience's interests and needs. Imagine you're passionate about fitness and have a blog dedicated to workout routines and healthy living. Promoting fitness equipment, nutritional supplements, or online workout programs would make perfect sense. Your audience trusts you for advice in this area, and they're more likely to purchase products you genuinely recommend.

Creating content that resonates with your audience is another key aspect. Your content should educate, entertain, and inspire. Whether you're writing a blog post, recording a video, or posting on social media, your goal is to add value. For instance, instead of just writing a review of a product, share a personal story about how it helped you solve a problem or achieve a

Chapter 1: What is Affiliate Marketing?

goal. Authenticity is your best ally; people can tell when you're being genuine, and they're more likely to trust your recommendations.

SEO, or search engine optimization, is your secret weapon in driving organic traffic to your content. By understanding what your audience is searching for and optimizing your content accordingly, you can attract more visitors to your site without spending a dime on advertising. This involves researching keywords, creating high-quality content around those keywords, and building backlinks from reputable sites.

Social media can amplify your reach even further. Platforms like Instagram, YouTube, and TikTok are perfect for visual storytelling and connecting with your audience on a personal level. By engaging with your followers, sharing valuable content, and showcasing products in a natural, authentic

Chapter 1: What is Affiliate Marketing?

way, you can drive significant traffic to your affiliate links.

Transparency and trust are the foundation of successful affiliate marketing. Always disclose your affiliate relationships. Not only is it a legal requirement, but it also builds trust with your audience. People appreciate honesty and are more likely to support you if they know you're earning a commission from your recommendations.

In essence, affiliate marketing is about building relationships—between you and your audience, and between your audience and the products they need. It's about creating content that adds value, solves problems, and inspires action. It's a journey that requires patience, persistence, and a genuine passion for helping others. But with the right approach, the rewards can be substantial.

Chapter 1: What is Affiliate Marketing?

As you embark on this journey, remember that success doesn't come overnight. It takes time to build trust, create valuable content, and attract a loyal audience. But with dedication and a focus on providing real value, you can turn affiliate marketing into a thriving, sustainable business.

So, are you ready to dive in and start your affiliate marketing journey? It's time to explore, learn, and grow. The possibilities are endless, and the potential rewards are within your reach. Let's get started.

Chapter 2:
The Magic of Affiliate Marketing:

The magic of affiliate marketing lies in its ability to transform ordinary moments into extraordinary opportunities. Imagine a world where your passion for a topic becomes the gateway to financial freedom, where your insights and recommendations not only help others but also create a steady stream of income for you. That's the allure of affiliate marketing—an alchemy of content, connection, and commerce.

At its heart, affiliate marketing is about relationships. It's about the trust you build with your audience and the trust you place in the products you promote. Unlike traditional advertising, which often feels impersonal and intrusive, affiliate marketing thrives on authenticity and personal endorsement. Your recommendations carry weight because they

Chapter 2: The Magic of Affiliate Marketing

come from a place of genuine enthusiasm and experience.

Consider the scenario where you've just stumbled upon a fantastic product that has made a significant difference in your life. Perhaps it's a fitness gadget that's helped you stay on track with your health goals or a software tool that's streamlined your business operations. The natural inclination is to share this discovery with others, to spread the word about something that genuinely works. Affiliate marketing channels this instinct, allowing you to share your positive experiences while earning a commission for every sale made through your referral.

The magic unfolds when you realize that your influence extends far beyond your immediate circle. Through your blog, YouTube channel, or social media platforms, you can reach a global audience. People

Chapter 2: The Magic of Affiliate Marketing

from different corners of the world, who share your interests and face similar challenges, find your content and take your recommendations seriously. This global reach means that your earning potential is not confined to a specific geography or time zone. Your content continues to work for you, generating income even while you sleep.

The beauty of affiliate marketing also lies in its low barrier to entry. Unlike traditional businesses that require substantial capital investment, affiliate marketing allows you to start with minimal financial outlay. Your primary investment is your time and effort in creating valuable content and building your online presence. This democratizes the opportunity, making it accessible to anyone with the passion and persistence to succeed.

Moreover, affiliate marketing leverages the power of passive income. Once you've set

Chapter 2: The Magic of Affiliate Marketing

up your content and embedded your affiliate links, your work continues to yield results long after the initial effort. This passive income potential is what makes affiliate marketing so attractive. It's about working smarter, not harder, and letting your content do the heavy lifting.

There's also a profound satisfaction in knowing that you're helping others make informed decisions. In a world inundated with choices, your insights and reviews provide clarity. You become a trusted advisor, guiding your audience towards products that genuinely enhance their lives. This sense of purpose adds a deeper dimension to your affiliate marketing endeavors, transforming it from a mere income-generating activity into a meaningful pursuit.

As you delve deeper into the world of affiliate marketing, you'll discover that it's a

Chapter 2: The Magic of Affiliate Marketing

dynamic and evolving field. There's always something new to learn, whether it's mastering the latest SEO techniques, understanding consumer behavior, or keeping up with emerging trends. This continuous learning process keeps the journey exciting and ensures that you're always growing, both personally and professionally.

The connections you make along the way are another magical aspect of affiliate marketing. You'll meet fellow marketers, engage with your audience, and form partnerships with brands. These connections can open doors to new opportunities, collaborations, and even friendships. The sense of community within the affiliate marketing world is strong, and there's a collective spirit of sharing knowledge and supporting each other's growth.

Chapter 2: The Magic of Affiliate Marketing

In essence, the magic of affiliate marketing lies in its blend of creativity, strategy, and human connection. It's about turning your passions into profits, building trust and credibility, and making a positive impact on the lives of others. It's a journey that requires dedication and patience, but the rewards—both tangible and intangible—are well worth the effort.

So, as you embark on this exciting path, embrace the magic that affiliate marketing offers. Let your passion shine through your content, build genuine connections with your audience, and enjoy the journey of turning your recommendations into a thriving source of income. The possibilities are endless, and the magic is real. It's time to discover it for yourself.

Chapter 3: Finding Your Passion

Chapter 3: Finding Your Passion:

Finding your passion with affiliate marketing is like discovering a hidden treasure within yourself. It's about aligning your interests, skills, and values with the products and services you promote, creating a harmonious blend that resonates with both you and your audience. This journey of self-discovery and alignment not only makes the process of affiliate marketing more enjoyable but also significantly increases your chances of success.

Passion is the fuel that drives your efforts, the spark that ignites your creativity and persistence. In the vast world of affiliate marketing, passion is what sets you apart. It transforms your content from mere information to a compelling narrative that engages and inspires. When you are genuinely passionate about the products you

Chapter 3: Finding Your Passion

promote, it shows. Your enthusiasm becomes contagious, your recommendations authentic, and your audience can feel your excitement.

The first step in finding your passion with affiliate marketing is to look inward. Reflect on your interests and hobbies. What topics do you find yourself constantly drawn to? What activities make you lose track of time because you're so immersed in them? Your passions are often hidden in these moments of deep engagement and joy. For instance, if you love cooking and experimenting with new recipes, a food blog where you promote kitchen gadgets and gourmet ingredients could be a natural fit. Similarly, if you're a fitness enthusiast, promoting workout gear, supplements, and training programs might resonate deeply with you.

Understanding your strengths and skills is equally important. Passion alone is not

Chapter 3: Finding Your Passion

enough; you need to be able to communicate your passion effectively. What are you good at? Do you have a knack for writing engaging blog posts, creating captivating videos, or connecting with people on social media? Leveraging your strengths will help you create high-quality content that stands out and attracts an audience. If you're an excellent storyteller, you can weave personal anecdotes and experiences into your content, making it relatable and compelling. If you're a tech-savvy individual, creating in-depth product reviews and tutorials could be your forte.

Your values also play a crucial role in finding your passion with affiliate marketing. Promoting products that align with your values and beliefs creates a sense of integrity and trust. It's not just about making money; it's about making a positive impact. If sustainability and eco-friendliness are important to you, promoting green

Chapter 3: Finding Your Passion

products and brands that prioritize ethical practices will resonate not only with you but also with a growing audience that shares those values. This alignment between your values and the products you promote enhances your credibility and builds a loyal following.

Once you've identified your passions, strengths, and values, the next step is to explore the market. Research potential niches and see where your interests intersect with audience demand. This is where the magic happens. When your passion aligns with a profitable niche, you hit the sweet spot. For instance, if you're passionate about travel and have a knack for photography, promoting travel gear, accessories, and even travel insurance could be a lucrative niche. Look for gaps in the market where you can offer unique insights and value.

Chapter 3: Finding Your Passion

Creating content around your passion is a deeply fulfilling experience. It doesn't feel like work because you're doing what you love. Your content becomes a reflection of your journey, your growth, and your discoveries. It's about sharing your passion with the world, helping others, and making a difference. This authenticity and genuine enthusiasm attract like-minded individuals who share your interests and values, building a community around your content.

Engaging with your audience is another critical aspect of finding your passion with affiliate marketing. Your passion will naturally draw people who resonate with your message. Interact with them, listen to their feedback, and understand their needs and preferences. This connection not only helps you refine your content but also strengthens the bond with your audience. They become more than just followers; they become part of your journey, your tribe.

Chapter 3: Finding Your Passion

As you immerse yourself in your passion, you'll find that challenges become opportunities for growth. Your passion fuels your perseverance, helping you navigate the ups and downs of affiliate marketing. It keeps you motivated to learn, adapt, and innovate. Every setback becomes a learning experience, every success a testament to your dedication and love for what you do.

In the end, finding your passion with affiliate marketing is about more than just making money. It's about creating a fulfilling and meaningful career that aligns with who you are. It's about waking up every day excited to share your knowledge, help others, and make a positive impact. It's about building a legacy that reflects your passions, strengths, and values. And most importantly, it's about enjoying the journey, knowing that you're doing what you love and loving what you do.

Chapter 3: Finding Your Passion

So, as you embark on this path, remember that your passion is your greatest asset. Embrace it, nurture it, and let it guide you. The possibilities are endless, and the rewards are beyond measure. This is the magic of affiliate marketing—turning your passions into a thriving, fulfilling career.

Chapter 4: The Hunt for the Right Affiliate Programs

Chapter 4:
The Hunt for the Right Affiliate Programs:

Embarking on the hunt for the right affiliate marketing program is akin to setting out on an exhilarating treasure hunt. It's a journey filled with discovery, analysis, and strategic decisions, ultimately leading you to the perfect partnership that aligns with your goals and passions. This chapter delves into the intricate process of finding an affiliate marketing program that not only fits your niche but also propels you toward success.

The initial step in this quest is to understand the vast landscape of affiliate marketing programs available. The digital realm is teeming with options, each offering a unique set of features, commission structures, and support systems. It's essential to have a clear

Chapter 4: The Hunt for the Right Affiliate Programs

vision of what you want to achieve and the kind of products or services you want to promote. Your passion and expertise should guide this decision, ensuring that the programs you consider align with your interests and strengths.

As you delve into this exploration, it's crucial to immerse yourself in research. Begin by identifying the major players in your niche. Look at what other successful affiliates are promoting and the programs they are part of. This provides valuable insights into what works in your chosen field. However, don't limit yourself to the obvious choices. Sometimes, the hidden gems—lesser-known programs with excellent products and competitive commissions—offer the best opportunities.

Understanding the terms and conditions of each program is vital. This is where the fine

Chapter 4: The Hunt for the Right Affiliate Programs

print comes into play. Dive deep into the commission structures to grasp how and when you will be paid. Some programs offer high commissions but may have stringent requirements or long payment cycles, while others might provide lower commissions but with easier terms and faster payouts. Analyze which model suits your financial goals and operational capabilities.

In your hunt, the reputation of the affiliate program is a crucial factor. A program's credibility can significantly impact your success. Seek out reviews, testimonials, and case studies from other affiliates. Forums, social media groups, and affiliate marketing communities can be invaluable resources for this kind of insider information. A program with a solid reputation is likely to offer better support, more reliable payments, and a higher quality of products or services, all of which contribute to your success.

Chapter 4: The Hunt for the Right Affiliate Programs

One aspect that often distinguishes a good program from a great one is the quality of the support provided to affiliates. A responsive and knowledgeable affiliate manager can be a game-changer, offering guidance, resources, and personalized advice to help you maximize your earnings. Evaluate the level of support available, from onboarding processes to ongoing assistance. Programs that invest in their affiliates' success tend to foster long-term, mutually beneficial relationships.

The hunt for the right affiliate marketing program also involves a thorough examination of the marketing resources provided. High-quality banners, creative assets, tracking tools, and promotional materials can significantly enhance your marketing efforts. Programs that offer robust resources not only save you time but also

Chapter 4: The Hunt for the Right Affiliate Programs

ensure that your promotional efforts are more effective and professional.

Once you've shortlisted potential programs, it's time to test the waters. Sign up for a few and start promoting their products. This hands-on experience is invaluable. Monitor your performance, track conversions, and assess how well these programs align with your audience. Pay attention to the ease of use of their platforms, the responsiveness of their support teams, and the overall experience of working with them. This trial period can reveal insights that no amount of research can provide.

A critical component of your hunt is the alignment of the program with your audience. Your success as an affiliate marketer hinges on promoting products that resonate with your followers. Pay close attention to how your audience responds to

Chapter 4: The Hunt for the Right Affiliate Programs

the products and services you're promoting. Engagement metrics, feedback, and sales data will give you a clear picture of what works and what doesn't. Programs that offer products your audience loves will naturally perform better, leading to higher commissions and a more loyal following.

Flexibility and scalability are also important considerations. As your affiliate marketing business grows, your needs will evolve. Programs that offer scalable solutions, such as tiered commission structures or bonuses for high performers, will better support your growth. Additionally, flexibility in marketing strategies—allowing you to promote products through various channels like blogs, social media, email marketing, and more—can enhance your reach and impact.

Chapter 4: The Hunt for the Right Affiliate Programs

Finally, trust your instincts. The hunt for the right affiliate marketing program is as much about intuition as it is about analysis. If a program feels right, if it aligns with your values, passions, and goals, it's worth pursuing. Your enthusiasm and confidence in the program will translate into more genuine and effective promotions, ultimately driving your success.

In conclusion, the hunt for the right affiliate marketing program is a dynamic and engaging process. It requires a blend of research, analysis, and intuition. By immersing yourself in this journey, understanding the intricacies of each program, and aligning your choices with your passions and audience, you'll uncover the perfect partnership that sets you on the path to affiliate marketing success. The thrill of the hunt, the satisfaction of discovery, and the excitement of forging new partnerships

Chapter 4: The Hunt for the Right Affiliate Programs

make this journey not just rewarding, but truly magical.

Chapter 5: Building Your Platform:

Building your affiliate marketing platform is a journey that combines creativity, strategy, and a deep understanding of your audience. It's more than just setting up a website or a blog; it's about creating a space where your passion meets the needs of your audience, fostering a community, and providing value that drives engagement and conversions.

The first step in building your platform is to choose the right medium. This decision should be guided by your strengths, interests, and where your audience spends their time. For many, a blog or a website serves as the cornerstone of their affiliate marketing efforts. It's a place where you can share in-depth content, reviews, and resources. Others might find that social media platforms, YouTube channels, or

Chapter 5: Building Your Platform

podcasts better suit their style and audience engagement.

Creating a compelling brand identity is crucial. Your brand is what sets you apart from countless other affiliates. It's your unique voice, your story, and the value you offer. Think about what makes you passionate about the products you promote and how you can convey that passion to your audience. Your brand should be consistent across all your platforms, from the colors and fonts you use to the tone and style of your content.

Content is the heart of your platform. High-quality, valuable content is what will attract and retain your audience. It's not just about pushing products; it's about providing solutions, answering questions, and becoming a trusted resource. Whether you're writing blog posts, creating videos, or recording podcasts, focus on delivering

Chapter 5: Building Your Platform

content that is informative, engaging, and relevant to your audience's needs.

SEO, or search engine optimization, is a critical component of building your platform. By optimizing your content for search engines, you can increase your visibility and attract organic traffic. This involves researching keywords that your target audience is searching for and incorporating them naturally into your content. It's also about understanding the technical aspects of SEO, such as site structure, load times, and mobile-friendliness, to ensure your platform is accessible and user-friendly.

Building a platform also involves creating an engaging and user-friendly design. Your website or blog should be easy to navigate, with clear categories, a search function, and intuitive menus. The design should be clean and professional, reflecting the quality of

Chapter 5: Building Your Platform

your content. For social media or YouTube, your profile should be well-organized, with a clear description, links to your other platforms, and a consistent posting schedule.

Interactivity and community-building are key elements of a successful affiliate marketing platform. Encourage your audience to engage with your content through comments, shares, and likes. Respond to their questions and feedback, and foster a sense of community. This not only builds loyalty but also increases the chances of your content being shared, expanding your reach.

Email marketing is another powerful tool in building your platform. By collecting email addresses and sending regular newsletters, you can keep your audience informed about new content, special promotions, and exclusive offers. Email marketing allows for a more personal connection with your

Chapter 5: Building Your Platform

audience and can drive significant traffic to your site or blog.

Monetizing your platform goes beyond affiliate links. Consider incorporating multiple revenue streams, such as sponsored posts, digital products, or memberships. Diversifying your income can provide more stability and increase your earnings potential. However, always prioritize providing value over making a quick profit. Your audience's trust and loyalty are your most valuable assets.

Analytics and continuous improvement are vital in building a successful platform. Regularly review your analytics to understand what content is performing well, where your traffic is coming from, and how your audience is engaging with your content. Use this data to refine your strategy, focusing on what works and improving what doesn't. Building an affiliate marketing

Chapter 5: Building Your Platform

platform is an ongoing process, and staying flexible and responsive to changes is crucial.

Finally, authenticity is at the core of a successful affiliate marketing platform. Be genuine in your promotions and transparent with your audience. Only promote products that you believe in and that you think will genuinely benefit your audience. Your honesty and integrity will build trust, and a trusted recommendation is far more valuable than a forced promotion.

In conclusion, building your affiliate marketing platform is a multifaceted endeavor that requires creativity, strategy, and a deep connection with your audience. By focusing on creating valuable content, optimizing for search engines, designing an engaging user experience, fostering community, leveraging email marketing, diversifying your income streams, and staying authentic, you can create a platform

Chapter 5: Building Your Platform

that not only drives affiliate sales but also builds a loyal and engaged audience. This journey is both challenging and rewarding, offering endless opportunities for growth and success in the affiliate marketing world.

Chapter 6:
Content is King:

In the realm of affiliate marketing, content truly is king. It's the cornerstone upon which successful campaigns are built and the engine that drives traffic, engagement, and conversions. But what does it mean to say that "content is king," and how can you harness the power of great content to achieve success in affiliate marketing? Let's explore this in depth.

At the heart of every successful affiliate marketing strategy is content that resonates with its audience. This content isn't just about promoting products; it's about providing value. When you create content that addresses the needs, desires, and pain points of your audience, you build trust and establish yourself as an authority in your niche. This trust is crucial because people

Chapter 6: Content is King

are more likely to purchase products recommended by someone they see as a credible source.

Creating high-quality content requires a deep understanding of your audience. Who are they? What are their interests, problems, and needs? What kind of content do they consume, and where do they consume it? Answering these questions allows you to tailor your content to fit your audience perfectly. This might mean writing in-depth blog posts, creating engaging videos, or producing informative podcasts. The medium is less important than the relevance and value of the content itself.

Quality content is also about storytelling. People are naturally drawn to stories because they are relatable and memorable. When you weave your affiliate promotions into compelling narratives, you create a connection with your audience. Instead of

Chapter 6: Content is King

just listing the features of a product, tell a story about how it helped solve a problem or improved someone's life. This approach makes your content more engaging and persuasive.

SEO, or search engine optimization, is another critical aspect of content creation. Great content needs to be discoverable, and that's where SEO comes in. By optimizing your content for search engines, you increase the chances of it being found by people searching for information related to your niche. This involves using relevant keywords, creating descriptive meta tags, and ensuring your content is well-structured and easy to read. SEO is a way to amplify the reach of your content, bringing more potential customers to your site.

Consistency in content creation is essential. Building a loyal audience requires regular updates and fresh content. This doesn't

Chapter 6: Content is King

mean you need to churn out content daily, but you should have a consistent schedule that your audience can rely on. This consistency keeps your audience engaged and coming back for more, which is crucial for maintaining and growing your traffic over time.

Engagement is another critical component of effective content. Your content should encourage interaction, whether that's through comments, shares, likes, or other forms of feedback. This interaction not only boosts your visibility but also provides valuable insights into what your audience cares about. Responding to comments and engaging with your audience fosters a sense of community and loyalty, which can significantly enhance your affiliate marketing efforts.

Diversifying your content can also be beneficial. While blog posts and articles are

Chapter 6: Content is King

foundational, incorporating videos, infographics, and other multimedia elements can make your content more engaging and accessible. Different people consume content in different ways, so offering a variety of formats can help you reach a broader audience.

Monetizing your content through affiliate links should be done thoughtfully. The key is to integrate these links naturally into your content. They should feel like a helpful suggestion rather than a hard sell. When you genuinely recommend products that you believe in and that align with your content, your audience is more likely to trust your recommendations and make a purchase.

Analytics play a crucial role in refining your content strategy. By regularly reviewing your analytics, you can see which content is performing well and which isn't. This data allows you to make informed decisions

Chapter 6: Content is King

about what types of content to produce more of and what to improve. It's an ongoing process of optimization that ensures your content continues to meet the needs of your audience.

Finally, authenticity is the foundation of effective content. In an age where consumers are bombarded with advertisements and promotions, authenticity stands out. Be honest about your experiences with the products you promote. If there are downsides, mention them. Transparency builds trust, and trust leads to long-term success in affiliate marketing.

In summary, content is indeed king in the world of affiliate marketing. By creating high-quality, valuable content that resonates with your audience, optimizing it for search engines, engaging with your audience, and maintaining authenticity, you can build a successful affiliate marketing platform. This

Chapter 6: Content is King

approach not only drives traffic and conversions but also builds a loyal and engaged community that trusts your recommendations and values your insights.

Chapter 7: Building Your Brand

Building a brand with affiliate marketing is an art that requires a deep understanding of your audience, consistency in your messaging, and a commitment to authenticity. When done correctly, it transforms your affiliate marketing efforts from mere transactions to a trusted relationship with your audience. Here's how to master this art and create a brand that stands out in the crowded online space.

To build a successful brand, you must first understand the essence of what a brand is. It's not just a logo or a catchy slogan; it's the experience and perception people have when they interact with your content. It's the personality and values you project through your work. Your brand should reflect your core beliefs and resonate with the values of

Chapter 7: Building Your Brand

your audience. This connection is what fosters loyalty and trust.

The foundation of your brand is your story. This narrative is unique to you and can be a powerful tool in differentiating yourself from others. Why did you start your affiliate marketing journey? What challenges did you face, and how did you overcome them? Sharing your personal journey adds a layer of authenticity to your brand. It's this authenticity that helps you connect with your audience on a deeper level.

Consistency in your messaging and content is crucial. Your audience should know what to expect from you, whether it's through your blog posts, videos, or social media updates. This consistency builds familiarity and trust. It's about maintaining a steady voice, style, and tone across all your platforms. When your audience encounters

Chapter 7: Building Your Brand

your content, they should immediately recognize it as yours.

Creating valuable content is at the heart of building your brand. Each piece of content you produce should aim to educate, entertain, or solve a problem for your audience. This positions you as an authority in your niche and encourages people to return to you for more insights and recommendations. When your audience feels that you genuinely care about providing value, they're more likely to trust your affiliate recommendations.

Engagement with your audience is another critical aspect. This interaction goes beyond just responding to comments; it's about fostering a community. Ask for feedback, encourage discussions, and be approachable. Showing that you value your audience's opinions and contributions helps to build a loyal following. People want to feel heard

Chapter 7: Building Your Brand

and appreciated, and when you create that environment, your brand strengthens.

Visual identity plays a significant role in brand building. While it's true that your brand is more than just a logo, having a cohesive visual identity helps to establish a professional and recognizable presence. Choose a color palette, typography, and design elements that reflect your brand's personality. These visual cues should be consistent across your website, social media profiles, and any other platforms you use.

Transparency and honesty are non-negotiable in building a brand with affiliate marketing. Disclose your affiliate relationships clearly and honestly. Your audience respects and trusts you more when you are upfront about earning commissions. They understand that you need to make a living, and they're more likely to support

Chapter 7: Building Your Brand

you if they see you as honest and transparent.

Building partnerships and collaborations can also elevate your brand. Partnering with other influencers or brands in your niche can help you reach new audiences and add value to your existing followers. Choose partners whose values align with yours to ensure a cohesive message. Collaborations can take many forms, from guest posts and joint webinars to co-created products or services.

Regularly evaluate and refine your brand strategy. The online space is dynamic, and it's essential to stay updated with trends and shifts in your niche. Use analytics to understand what content resonates most with your audience and where there might be gaps or opportunities. Continuously learning and adapting ensures that your brand remains relevant and effective.

Chapter 7: Building Your Brand

Finally, patience and persistence are key. Building a brand is not an overnight endeavor. It takes time to grow a loyal audience and establish yourself as a trusted authority. Stay committed to your vision, continue providing value, and your efforts will pay off.

In conclusion, building your brand with affiliate marketing is about more than just promoting products. It's about creating a unique identity that resonates with your audience, consistently providing valuable content, engaging authentically, and maintaining transparency. With these principles, you can create a brand that not only drives affiliate sales but also builds lasting relationships with your audience, leading to sustained success.

Chapter 8: The SEO Game

Chapter 8:
The SEO Game:

In the realm of affiliate marketing, the success of your efforts hinges on your ability to be discovered by potential customers. This is where Search Engine Optimization (SEO) comes into play. SEO is the art and science of enhancing your online content to achieve higher visibility in search engine results, thus driving organic traffic to your affiliate links. Understanding and mastering SEO is crucial to establishing a profitable affiliate marketing business.

SEO begins with understanding how search engines operate. These complex algorithms are designed to deliver the most relevant and authoritative content to users based on their search queries. By optimizing your content to align with these algorithms, you improve your chances of appearing at the top of

Chapter 8: The SEO Game

search results. This visibility is vital because most users do not look beyond the first page of search results.

Keywords are the cornerstone of SEO. These are the terms and phrases that potential customers use when searching for information, products, or services online. Identifying the right keywords involves thorough research to understand what your target audience is searching for. Tools like Google Keyword Planner, Ahrefs, and SEMrush can help uncover these valuable terms. Once identified, these keywords should be strategically incorporated into your content, including your titles, headings, and body text, without compromising the natural flow and readability of your content.

Creating high-quality, valuable content is the most important aspect of SEO. Search engines prioritize content that offers genuine value to users. This means your content

Chapter 8: The SEO Game

should be informative, engaging, and relevant to your audience's needs. When you provide answers to their questions and solutions to their problems, you not only attract search engines but also build trust and credibility with your audience. This trust is essential in affiliate marketing, as it influences your audience's willingness to follow your recommendations.

On-page optimization is another critical factor in SEO. This involves optimizing various elements of your website to improve its search engine ranking. Your title tags, meta descriptions, and headers should be optimized with your target keywords. Additionally, your content should be well-structured with clear headings and subheadings, making it easier for search engines to understand the hierarchy and context of your content. Images and videos should also be optimized with descriptive alt text and appropriate file names.

Chapter 8: The SEO Game

User experience (UX) plays a significant role in SEO as well. Search engines favor websites that offer a seamless and enjoyable experience for users. This includes fast loading times, mobile responsiveness, easy navigation, and a clean, clutter-free design. A positive user experience not only keeps visitors on your site longer but also reduces bounce rates, both of which signal to search engines that your site is valuable and worth promoting.

Building backlinks is a powerful SEO strategy. Backlinks are links from other websites that point to your content. They act as votes of confidence, signaling to search engines that your content is authoritative and trustworthy. Earning backlinks can be achieved through creating shareable, high-quality content that others want to link to, guest posting on reputable sites, and engaging in influencer outreach. The more

Chapter 8: The SEO Game

high-quality backlinks you have, the higher your content is likely to rank.

Social signals, although not a direct ranking factor, can influence your SEO efforts. When your content is shared and discussed on social media platforms, it increases its visibility and can attract more backlinks. Social media engagement can drive traffic to your site, which in turn can improve your search engine rankings. Therefore, an active social media presence can complement your SEO strategy and amplify your affiliate marketing success.

Regularly monitoring and analyzing your SEO performance is essential to maintaining and improving your rankings. Tools like Google Analytics and Google Search Console provide valuable insights into how your content is performing, what keywords are driving traffic, and where there are opportunities for improvement. By

Chapter 8: The SEO Game

continuously refining your SEO strategy based on these insights, you can stay ahead of the competition and sustain your visibility.

In conclusion, SEO is a vital component of affiliate marketing success. It involves a combination of keyword research, high-quality content creation, on-page optimization, user experience enhancement, backlink building, and social media engagement. By mastering these elements, you can achieve higher search engine rankings, attract more organic traffic, and ultimately, drive more conversions through your affiliate links. The investment in SEO pays off in the form of sustained visibility, credibility, and profitability in the competitive world of affiliate marketing.

Chapter 9: Social Media Savvy

Chapter 9:
Social Media Savvy:

In today's digital age, social media isn't just a platform for sharing personal updates and photos; it's a powerful tool that can significantly enhance your affiliate marketing success. Understanding how to leverage social media effectively is essential for reaching a broader audience, building relationships, and driving traffic to your affiliate links.

Being social media savvy starts with understanding the unique strengths and demographics of each platform. Facebook, Instagram, Twitter, LinkedIn, Pinterest, and TikTok each have distinct user bases and content styles. To be effective, you need to tailor your approach to fit each platform. This means understanding the type of content that performs well, the peak times

Chapter 9: Social Media Savvy

for engagement, and the nuances of each audience. For example, Instagram thrives on visually appealing content, while LinkedIn is better suited for professional, insightful posts.

Creating a compelling social media presence requires authenticity and consistency. People follow accounts that they find relatable, trustworthy, and valuable. By sharing content that reflects your personality, expertise, and genuine interest in your niche, you can build a loyal following. Consistency in posting helps keep your audience engaged and increases your visibility in their feeds. Regular updates, engaging stories, and interactive posts can help maintain and grow your follower base.

Engagement is the heart of social media. It's not enough to simply post content; you need to interact with your audience. Responding to comments, participating in discussions,

Chapter 9: Social Media Savvy

and acknowledging feedback shows that you value your followers. This interaction builds a sense of community and trust, which is crucial in affiliate marketing. When your audience feels connected to you, they are more likely to trust your recommendations and click on your affiliate links.

Visual content is particularly powerful on social media. High-quality images, graphics, and videos can capture attention and convey information quickly and effectively. Using tools like Canva or Adobe Spark, you can create eye-catching visuals that highlight the benefits of the products or services you are promoting. Tutorials, unboxings, and reviews in video format can be especially engaging and provide your audience with a closer look at what you are endorsing.

Storytelling is another vital component of a successful social media strategy. Sharing personal stories and experiences related to

Chapter 9: Social Media Savvy

the products you are promoting can make your recommendations more relatable and persuasive. Stories can highlight how a product has benefited you personally or solved a particular problem. This narrative approach not only makes your content more engaging but also helps build an emotional connection with your audience.

Collaborating with influencers and other content creators can amplify your reach and credibility. Partnering with individuals who have a strong following in your niche can introduce your content to a broader audience. These collaborations can take various forms, such as guest posts, joint giveaways, or co-hosted live sessions. By aligning yourself with trusted voices in your industry, you can enhance your reputation and attract more followers.

Running social media ads can also boost your affiliate marketing efforts. Platforms

Chapter 9: Social Media Savvy

like Facebook and Instagram offer targeted advertising options that allow you to reach specific demographics based on interests, behaviors, and location. Sponsored posts and stories can increase the visibility of your content and drive more traffic to your affiliate links. These ads should be crafted carefully to blend seamlessly with organic content and provide clear calls to action.

Analytics play a crucial role in refining your social media strategy. By monitoring metrics such as engagement rates, click-through rates, and follower growth, you can gain insights into what works and what doesn't. Platforms like Facebook Insights, Instagram Analytics, and Twitter Analytics provide valuable data that can help you understand your audience's preferences and optimize your content accordingly. Regularly reviewing these metrics and adjusting your approach ensures that your social media

Chapter 9: Social Media Savvy

efforts remain effective and aligned with your goals.

Social media is also a powerful tool for building your personal brand. Your profiles should reflect your brand's identity and values consistently. This includes using a cohesive color scheme, tone of voice, and messaging across all platforms. A strong personal brand enhances your credibility and makes you more recognizable to your audience. Over time, as people become familiar with your brand, they are more likely to trust your recommendations and engage with your content.

In conclusion, being social media savvy is essential for affiliate marketing success. It involves understanding the nuances of different platforms, creating authentic and engaging content, actively interacting with your audience, leveraging visual storytelling, collaborating with influencers,

Chapter 9: Social Media Savvy

using targeted ads, and continuously analyzing your performance. By mastering these elements, you can build a strong social media presence that drives traffic to your affiliate links, fosters trust with your audience, and ultimately, increases your profitability. Embrace the power of social media, and let it be the catalyst for your affiliate marketing triumphs.

Chapter 10: The Power of Email Marketing

Chapter 10:
The Power of Email Marketing:

In the realm of affiliate marketing, email marketing is a force to be reckoned with. Its potential to connect directly with your audience, foster relationships, and drive conversions is unparalleled. Unlike social media, where algorithms dictate visibility, email marketing allows you to reach your audience consistently, right in their inbox. Understanding how to harness this power can significantly enhance your affiliate marketing success.

The magic of email marketing lies in its ability to create a personalized experience for each subscriber. When someone joins your email list, they are granting you permission to communicate with them directly. This level of access is a privilege and should be treated with care. Every email

Chapter 10: The Power of Email Marketing

you send should aim to add value, whether through informative content, exclusive offers, or personal insights. This value-driven approach helps build trust and loyalty, essential components for successful affiliate marketing.

Crafting compelling emails starts with understanding your audience. Knowing their interests, pain points, and preferences allows you to tailor your messages to resonate with them. Segmentation is a powerful tool in this regard. By dividing your email list into smaller groups based on specific criteria, you can send targeted emails that speak directly to the needs of each segment. For instance, if you are promoting different products, you can segment your list based on past purchase behavior or expressed interests, ensuring that your recommendations are relevant.

Chapter 10: The Power of Email Marketing

The subject line is your first point of contact and plays a crucial role in whether your email gets opened. It should be engaging, intriguing, and give a glimpse of what the reader can expect. A well-crafted subject line piques curiosity and encourages the recipient to open the email. Once they do, the content inside must deliver on the promise made in the subject line. Clear, concise, and compelling content keeps readers engaged and more likely to act on your recommendations.

Personalization goes beyond just using the recipient's name. It involves crafting messages that feel unique to the reader. Sharing personal stories, addressing common challenges, and offering tailored solutions can make your emails feel more like a conversation and less like a sales pitch. This personal touch builds a connection with your audience, making them more receptive to your affiliate links.

Chapter 10: The Power of Email Marketing

Consistency is key in email marketing. Regular communication helps keep you top of mind for your subscribers. However, it's essential to strike a balance between staying in touch and overwhelming your audience. A consistent schedule, whether weekly, bi-weekly, or monthly, helps set expectations and keeps your audience engaged without feeling bombarded.

Automation is a powerful feature of email marketing that can enhance your affiliate marketing efforts. Automated email sequences, or drip campaigns, allow you to nurture leads over time. For example, when someone subscribes to your list, you can set up a series of welcome emails that introduce them to your brand, provide valuable content, and gradually introduce affiliate offers. These sequences work in the background, building relationships and

Chapter 10: The Power of Email Marketing

driving conversions without requiring constant manual effort.

One of the most significant advantages of email marketing is its measurable nature. Open rates, click-through rates, and conversion rates provide valuable insights into how your emails are performing. Analyzing these metrics helps you understand what resonates with your audience and what doesn't, allowing you to refine your strategy over time. A/B testing different subject lines, email formats, and calls to action can also help optimize your emails for better engagement and conversions.

The power of email marketing is amplified by its ability to drive traffic to your affiliate offers. Including clear and compelling calls to action in your emails directs readers to your affiliate links. Whether it's a product review, a special offer, or an informative

Chapter 10: The Power of Email Marketing

article, guiding your audience to take the next step is crucial. Well-placed links and buttons can significantly increase click-through rates and, ultimately, conversions.

Building a strong email list is foundational to email marketing success. Offering valuable incentives, such as free e-books, exclusive content, or special discounts, can encourage people to subscribe to your list. Promoting your email list across your website, social media channels, and other marketing platforms helps attract a steady stream of new subscribers. Once they're on your list, nurturing these relationships through valuable and relevant content ensures long-term engagement.

The trust factor in email marketing cannot be overstated. When your subscribers trust you, they are more likely to take your recommendations seriously. Building this

Chapter 10: The Power of Email Marketing

trust takes time and consistency. Sharing genuine experiences, providing honest reviews, and being transparent about your affiliate relationships fosters trust and credibility. When your audience feels confident that you have their best interests at heart, they are more likely to act on your affiliate links.

In conclusion, the power of email marketing in affiliate marketing lies in its ability to create personalized, direct, and consistent communication with your audience. By understanding your audience, crafting compelling and personalized content, maintaining consistency, leveraging automation, analyzing performance, driving traffic, building a strong list, and fostering trust, you can significantly enhance your affiliate marketing success. Embrace the power of email marketing, and let it be the catalyst for building lasting relationships and driving substantial affiliate revenue.

Chapter 11:
Transparency and Trust:

Certainly! Trust and transparency are the cornerstone of successful affiliate marketing. In an online world saturated with promotional content, establishing genuine connections with your audience is more critical than ever. Let's delve into why trust and transparency are not just desirable but indispensable elements for your affiliate marketing success.

Building Trust Through Authenticity:

Trust begins with authenticity. When you share your genuine experiences, insights, and opinions, your audience perceives you as credible and trustworthy. Authenticity humanizes your brand and fosters a connection with your audience that goes beyond transactional relationships. Whether

Chapter 11: Transparency and Trust

you're recommending products, sharing tips, or discussing industry trends, authenticity builds a foundation of trust that encourages your audience to listen to your recommendations and act upon them.

Transparency in Affiliate Relationships:

Transparency is equally vital in affiliate marketing. Being transparent about your affiliate relationships establishes integrity and honesty with your audience. Clearly disclosing when you stand to earn a commission from a recommendation not only complies with legal requirements but also demonstrates respect for your audience's intelligence. Transparency builds credibility and reassures your audience that your recommendations are driven by genuine belief in the product's value, rather than financial gain alone.

Chapter 11: Transparency and Trust

Honesty in Reviews and Recommendations:

Honesty is non-negotiable in affiliate marketing. Your audience relies on your recommendations to make informed purchasing decisions. Providing honest reviews, highlighting both strengths and weaknesses of products, enhances your credibility. When your audience trusts that you prioritize their interests over profit, they are more likely to consider your recommendations genuine and valuable.

Consistency and Reliability:

Consistency reinforces trust in affiliate marketing. Consistently delivering valuable content, maintaining ethical standards, and fulfilling promises to your audience builds reliability. When your audience knows they can count on you for unbiased advice and genuine recommendations, they are more

Chapter 11: Transparency and Trust

likely to trust your judgment and engage with your affiliate links.

Engaging Responsively with Your Audience:

Engaging responsively with your audience is another crucial aspect of building trust. Responding to questions, addressing concerns, and actively participating in discussions demonstrate your commitment to building meaningful relationships. By listening to your audience's feedback and incorporating their input, you show that their opinions matter, further strengthening trust and loyalty.

Transparency Beyond Affiliate Relationships:

Transparency extends beyond affiliate relationships to encompass all aspects of your online presence. Clearly

Chapter 11: Transparency and Trust

communicating your brand values, privacy policies, and any potential conflicts of interest enhances transparency. When your audience feels informed and respected, they are more likely to trust your recommendations and continue engaging with your content.

Building Long-Term Relationships:

Ultimately, trust and transparency in affiliate marketing pave the way for building long-term relationships with your audience. Long-term relationships are built on mutual respect, honesty, and shared values. By consistently demonstrating authenticity, transparency, and honesty, you foster a loyal audience that not only trusts your recommendations but also advocates for your brand.

Chapter 11: Transparency and Trust

In conclusion, trust and transparency are not just ethical imperatives but strategic advantages in affiliate marketing. By prioritizing authenticity, transparency in affiliate relationships, honesty in reviews, consistency, responsiveness, and comprehensive transparency, you cultivate a loyal audience that trusts your recommendations and values your expertise. Embrace trust and transparency as guiding principles in your affiliate marketing journey, and watch as they become the bedrock of your success.

Incorporate these principles into your affiliate marketing strategy, and you'll build a reputation as a trustworthy authority in your niche, setting yourself apart in a competitive marketplace. Trust and transparency are not mere ideals but practical strategies for sustainable affiliate marketing success.

Chapter 12: Analyzing and Optimizing

Chapter 12: Analyzing and Optimizing:

Absolutely! Analyzing and optimizing your affiliate marketing business is crucial for maximizing revenue and refining your strategies over time. Let's explore how you can effectively analyze and optimize your affiliate marketing efforts to achieve long-term success.

Understanding Your Metrics:

Successful optimization begins with a deep understanding of your metrics. Key performance indicators (KPIs) such as click-through rates (CTR), conversion rates, average order value (AOV), and revenue per click (RPC) provide valuable insights into the effectiveness of your campaigns. Analyzing these metrics allows you to identify strengths and weaknesses, pinpoint areas for improvement, and make

Chapter 12: Analyzing and Optimizing

data-driven decisions to optimize your performance.

Tracking and Attribution:

Accurate tracking and attribution are essential for understanding which channels, campaigns, and strategies drive the most conversions. Utilizing tracking tools such as Google Analytics, affiliate network analytics, and custom tracking parameters ensures you capture comprehensive data on user behavior and campaign performance. By attributing conversions correctly to each touchpoint in the customer journey, you can allocate resources effectively and optimize campaigns that deliver the highest return on investment (ROI).

Chapter 12: Analyzing and Optimizing

Segmenting and Targeting Your Audience:

Segmenting your audience based on demographics, behaviors, and interests allows for more targeted and personalized marketing efforts. Analyze customer data to identify segments that respond best to specific offers or content types. Tailoring your messaging and promotions to resonate with each segment increases relevance and engagement, driving higher conversion rates and maximizing revenue potential.

Content Performance and Optimization:

Content lies at the heart of affiliate marketing success. Analyzing the performance of your content—whether blog posts, reviews, videos, or social media posts—provides insights into what resonates most with your audience. Monitor metrics

Chapter 12: Analyzing and Optimizing

such as engagement metrics (likes, shares, comments), time on page, bounce rate, and conversion rates associated with each piece of content. Optimize content by refining headlines, improving readability, updating outdated information, and incorporating relevant keywords to enhance SEO performance and attract more qualified traffic.

Testing and Experimentation:

Continuous testing and experimentation are key to optimization. A/B testing different elements such as headlines, call-to-action (CTA) buttons, visuals, and promotional strategies allow you to identify which variations drive the best results. Test one variable at a time to isolate its impact on performance and make informed decisions based on data-driven insights. Implement successful findings across your campaigns

Chapter 12: Analyzing and Optimizing

to continuously improve conversion rates and maximize affiliate revenue.

Affiliate Program Analysis:

Evaluate the performance of your affiliate programs regularly to ensure alignment with your goals and objectives. Assess factors such as commission structure, cookie duration, product relevance, and affiliate support. Identify top-performing affiliates and nurture those relationships through personalized communication, exclusive offers, and strategic collaborations. Continuously seek new affiliate partnerships that align with your audience's interests and expand your reach in untapped markets.

Optimization Across Channels:

Diversifying your marketing channels and optimizing across multiple platforms—such as website content, email marketing, social

Chapter 12: Analyzing and Optimizing

media, and paid advertising—enhances your overall affiliate marketing strategy. Analyze channel-specific metrics to understand which platforms drive the most traffic, conversions, and revenue. Allocate resources based on channel performance and adapt strategies to capitalize on emerging trends and consumer behavior shifts.

Compliance and Ethical Considerations:

Maintaining compliance with legal regulations and ethical standards is essential for long-term success in affiliate marketing. Familiarize yourself with FTC guidelines regarding disclosure of affiliate relationships and ensure transparency in your promotional practices. Upholding ethical standards builds trust with your audience and strengthens your reputation as a credible affiliate marketer.

Chapter 12: Analyzing and Optimizing

Iterative Improvement and Adaptation:

Optimization is an ongoing process that requires iterative improvement and adaptation to evolving market trends and consumer preferences. Stay informed about industry developments, competitor strategies, and technological advancements that impact affiliate marketing. Embrace a mindset of continuous learning and experimentation to stay ahead of the curve and position yourself as a leader in your niche.

In conclusion, analyzing and optimizing your affiliate marketing business is essential for maximizing profitability, refining your strategies, and achieving sustainable growth. By understanding your metrics, tracking attribution, segmenting your audience, optimizing content performance, testing and experimenting, evaluating affiliate

Chapter 12: Analyzing and Optimizing

programs, optimizing across channels, maintaining compliance, and embracing iterative improvement, you can drive significant improvements in your affiliate marketing ROI.

Commit to a data-driven approach, prioritize audience engagement and satisfaction, and continuously refine your strategies to adapt to changing market dynamics. By consistently optimizing your affiliate marketing efforts, you'll build a resilient business that thrives in a competitive landscape.

Chapter 13: Scaling Up

Chapter 13:
Scaling Up:

Certainly! Scaling up your affiliate marketing business requires strategic planning, execution, and continuous optimization. Here's a detailed exploration of how you can effectively scale your affiliate marketing efforts to achieve substantial growth and profitability.

Strategic Planning for Growth:

Scaling your affiliate marketing business begins with strategic planning. Define clear, measurable goals that align with your long-term vision and objectives. Assess your current resources, capabilities, and market opportunities to identify areas for expansion. Develop a scalable business model that allows you to increase revenue without proportional increases in costs. Set realistic

Chapter 13: Scaling Up

milestones and timelines to track progress and adjust strategies as needed.

Expanding Your Audience Reach:

Expanding your audience reach is fundamental to scaling your affiliate marketing business. Identify new target demographics, niches, or geographic markets that align with your product offerings and affiliate partnerships. Utilize market research, audience segmentation, and competitive analysis to refine your targeting strategies. Invest in organic and paid acquisition channels to increase brand visibility, attract qualified traffic, and expand your reach across multiple platforms.

Leveraging Data-Driven Insights:

Data-driven insights play a pivotal role in scaling your affiliate marketing efforts. Continuously analyze performance metrics,

Chapter 13: Scaling Up

conversion rates, customer behavior, and ROI across all marketing channels. Use analytics tools and tracking platforms to gain actionable insights into which campaigns, content types, and promotional strategies yield the highest returns. Optimize underperforming campaigns, reallocate resources based on data-driven decisions, and capitalize on high-converting opportunities to maximize profitability.

Scaling Affiliate Partnerships:

Nurturing and expanding your affiliate partnerships is essential for scaling your affiliate marketing business. Identify top-performing affiliates who consistently drive quality traffic and conversions. Foster strong relationships through personalized communication, performance incentives, and strategic collaborations. Offer exclusive promotions, tailored content, and affiliate training programs to empower partners and enhance their effectiveness. Continuously

Chapter 13: Scaling Up

recruit new affiliates who align with your brand values and target audience to diversify your promotional reach and maximize affiliate-generated revenue.

Automation and Efficiency:

Automation and efficiency are key enablers of scalability in affiliate marketing. Implement marketing automation tools, CRM systems, and workflow automation solutions to streamline repetitive tasks, optimize resource allocation, and enhance productivity. Automate email marketing campaigns, content distribution, and affiliate payouts to reduce manual effort and scale operations seamlessly as your business grows. Leverage technology to track and analyze performance in real-time, identify opportunities for optimization, and maintain agility in a dynamic marketplace.

Chapter 13: Scaling Up

Scaling Content Strategy:

A robust content strategy is foundational to scaling your affiliate marketing business. Create high-quality, relevant content that resonates with your target audience and drives engagement. Develop an editorial calendar to plan and schedule content across multiple platforms, including blog posts, videos, social media, and email newsletters. Optimize content for SEO to increase organic traffic and improve search engine rankings. Experiment with different content formats, storytelling techniques, and multimedia elements to diversify your content portfolio and attract new audiences.

Continuous Learning and Innovation:

Continuous learning and innovation are essential for sustaining growth and competitiveness in affiliate marketing. Stay abreast of industry trends, technological

Chapter 13: Scaling Up

advancements, and evolving consumer behavior patterns. Attend conferences, webinars, and workshops to gain insights from industry experts and thought leaders. Experiment with emerging technologies, such as AI-driven analytics, augmented reality (AR), and voice search optimization, to stay ahead of the curve and differentiate your affiliate marketing strategies. Foster a culture of innovation within your team and encourage creativity, experimentation, and knowledge sharing to drive continuous improvement and innovation.

Scaling Operational Infrastructure:

Scaling your operational infrastructure is crucial to support growth and scalability in affiliate marketing. Invest in scalable hosting solutions, secure payment gateways, and robust cybersecurity measures to safeguard customer data and ensure operational reliability. Enhance customer support capabilities to deliver exceptional

Chapter 13: Scaling Up

service and foster long-term customer loyalty. Develop scalable processes and workflows for campaign management, affiliate recruitment, reporting, and performance analysis. Anticipate future scalability challenges and proactively invest in infrastructure upgrades, personnel training, and strategic partnerships to sustain growth and optimize operational efficiency.

In conclusion, scaling up your affiliate marketing business requires strategic planning, data-driven insights, audience expansion, affiliate partnership growth, automation, efficient operations, content strategy optimization, continuous learning, and innovation. By implementing these strategies, you can achieve sustainable growth, maximize profitability, and position your affiliate marketing business for long-term success in a competitive marketplace.

Chapter 13: Scaling Up

Commit to a systematic approach, prioritize scalability initiatives, and adapt your strategies based on market dynamics and performance metrics. Embrace scalability as a continuous journey of improvement and optimization, and leverage your strengths to capitalize on new opportunities for expansion and innovation in affiliate marketing.

Chapter 14: Overcoming Challenges

Chapter 14: Overcoming Challenges:

Certainly! Overcoming challenges in your affiliate marketing business requires resilience, strategic thinking, and a proactive approach to problem-solving. Here's a detailed exploration of how you can effectively navigate and conquer common challenges in affiliate marketing.

Affiliate marketing presents several challenges that can hinder your business growth and profitability. These challenges include:

1. Market Saturation and Competition:
   In a crowded marketplace, standing out among competitors can be challenging. Established affiliates and brands dominate search engine results and customer mindshare, making it difficult for newcomers to gain traction.

2. Changing Algorithms and Regulations:

Chapter 14: Overcoming Challenges

Search engine algorithms and advertising regulations often undergo updates, impacting your SEO rankings and advertising strategies. Staying compliant with regulatory changes while maintaining visibility requires adaptability and proactive monitoring.

3. Conversion Rate Optimization (CRO):
Converting visitors into paying customers is a fundamental goal in affiliate marketing. However, achieving high conversion rates requires continuous optimization of landing pages, user experience, and call-to-action strategies.

4. Quality Traffic Acquisition:
Generating quality traffic that converts into sales is crucial for affiliate success. However, acquiring targeted traffic through SEO, paid advertising, and content marketing strategies requires expertise and investment in analytics tools and marketing platforms.

Chapter 14: Overcoming Challenges

5. **Affiliate Network Management:
   Managing relationships with diverse affiliates, ensuring compliance with affiliate agreements, and optimizing performance can be complex. Maintaining transparency, effective communication, and fair commission structures are key to fostering strong partnerships.

Strategies to Overcome Challenges:

1. Differentiation and Niche Targeting:
   Differentiate your affiliate marketing business by focusing on a specific niche or audience segment. Conduct market research to identify underserved niches and tailor your content, products, and promotions to meet their specific needs. Position yourself as an expert in your niche to build trust and attract a loyal following.

2. Adaptability and Flexibility:
   Stay ahead of market trends and algorithm updates by continuously monitoring industry news and consumer

Chapter 14: Overcoming Challenges

behavior. Adapt your SEO strategies, content marketing efforts, and advertising campaigns to align with evolving best practices and regulatory requirements. Leverage data-driven insights to pivot quickly and capitalize on emerging opportunities.

3. Conversion Rate Optimization (CRO):
   Optimize your website's usability, navigation, and design to enhance user experience and increase conversion rates. Conduct A/B testing of landing pages, calls-to-action, and promotional offers to identify and implement strategies that resonate with your target audience. Utilize heatmaps, session recordings, and user feedback to gain actionable insights and refine your CRO efforts.

4. Diversified Traffic Sources:
   Reduce dependency on a single traffic source by diversifying your acquisition channels. Invest in SEO, paid advertising, social media marketing, email campaigns,

Chapter 14: Overcoming Challenges

and influencer partnerships to reach new audiences and drive qualified traffic to your affiliate offers. Analyze performance metrics to optimize channel mix and allocate resources effectively.

5. Relationship Building and Communication:
   Nurture strong relationships with affiliate partners, merchants, and industry influencers through regular communication, transparency, and mutual support. Collaborate on joint ventures, co-branded campaigns, and exclusive promotions to maximize exposure and reach. Provide affiliates with comprehensive training, promotional materials, and performance incentives to encourage engagement and loyalty.

6. Continuous Learning and Adaptation:
   Stay informed about industry trends, technological advancements, and competitive landscapes through continuous learning and professional development.

Chapter 14: Overcoming Challenges

Attend industry conferences, webinars, and workshops to network with peers, gain insights from industry leaders, and explore new growth opportunities. Embrace a growth mindset and prioritize innovation to stay ahead of the curve and maintain a competitive edge in affiliate marketing.

In conclusion, overcoming challenges in your affiliate marketing business requires a proactive mindset, strategic planning, and a commitment to continuous improvement. By understanding common challenges, implementing effective strategies, and fostering strong relationships, you can navigate obstacles, optimize performance, and achieve sustainable growth in affiliate marketing. Embrace challenges as opportunities for learning, innovation, and growth, and leverage your strengths to position your business for long-term success in a dynamic and competitive marketplace.

Chapter 15: Real Stories…Real Success

Chapter 15: Real Stories…Real Success

In the realm of affiliate marketing, amidst the sea of promotional content and advertisements, the authenticity and resonance of real stories have the power to captivate audiences, build trust, and drive meaningful engagement. As an affiliate marketer, harnessing the narrative potential of real stories can elevate your brand, establish deeper connections with your audience, and ultimately lead to sustainable success.

Understanding the Impact of Authenticity:

Authenticity forms the cornerstone of effective storytelling in affiliate marketing. When you share real stories, whether personal experiences or testimonials from satisfied customers, you humanize your brand and create a genuine connection with your audience. Unlike traditional sales pitches, which often focus solely on product features and benefits, real stories evoke emotions, inspire empathy, and foster trust.

Chapter 15: Real Stories...Real Success

Building Trust Through Personal Narratives:

Imagine you're promoting a fitness product through affiliate marketing. Instead of simply listing its specifications, consider sharing your own journey of transformation with the product. Describe how it helped you achieve your fitness goals, the challenges you faced along the way, and the tangible results you experienced. By weaving your personal narrative into the promotion, you not only demonstrate the product's efficacy but also position yourself as a relatable authority in your niche.

Leveraging Customer Testimonials and Case Studies:

Customer testimonials and case studies are powerful tools for leveraging real stories in affiliate marketing. Reach out to satisfied customers and invite them to share their experiences with the product or service. Highlight their success stories, challenges overcome, and how the product positively

Chapter 15: Real Stories...Real Success

impacted their lives. Authentic testimonials serve as social proof, reassuring potential buyers of the product's value and efficacy.

Crafting Compelling Content with Emotional Appeal:

Effective storytelling goes beyond factual information; it evokes emotions and resonates with the audience on a deeper level. When creating content, whether blog posts, videos, or social media updates, infuse your narrative with emotions such as joy, determination, or inspiration. Share anecdotes, milestones, and pivotal moments that illustrate the transformative power of the product or service you're promoting.

Connecting with Your Audience on a Personal Level:

One of the key advantages of using real stories in affiliate marketing is the ability to forge genuine connections with your audience. Authenticity breeds trust, and trust fosters loyalty. By sharing relatable stories and experiences, you invite your audience to

Chapter 15: Real Stories...Real Success
see themselves in your narrative. This connection not only increases engagement but also enhances the likelihood of conversion as your audience feels understood and valued.

Overcoming Challenges and Building Resilience:

While leveraging real stories can yield significant benefits, it's essential to navigate potential challenges such as privacy concerns, maintaining authenticity, and avoiding exaggeration. Respect your audience's trust by being transparent, honest, and ethical in your storytelling practices. Continuously evaluate the impact of your narratives and adapt your approach based on audience feedback and market trends.

Embracing the Authenticity Advantage:

In conclusion, the art of storytelling is a potent tool in your affiliate marketing arsenal. By embracing authenticity, sharing real stories, and connecting with your audience on a personal level, you can differentiate yourself in

Chapter 15: Real Stories...Real Success

a competitive marketplace, build a loyal following, and drive sustainable business growth. Remember, behind every successful affiliate marketing campaign lies a compelling narrative that resonates with hearts and minds, transcending mere sales pitches to inspire real action and loyalty.

Chapter 16: Your Affiliate Marketing Tool Box

Chapter 16:
Your Affiliate Marketing Tool Box:

In the dynamic world of affiliate marketing, having the right tools at your disposal can significantly enhance your productivity, efficiency, and overall success. These tools serve as your digital arsenal, empowering you to streamline processes, analyze data effectively, and optimize your marketing efforts for maximum impact. Here's a detailed look at the essential tools every affiliate marketer should consider:

1. Analytics and Tracking Software:

Analytics tools are the backbone of your affiliate marketing strategy, providing invaluable insights into campaign performance, audience behavior, and conversion metrics. Platforms like Google Analytics, Adobe Analytics, or

Chapter 16: Your Affiliate Marketing Tool Box

specialized affiliate marketing tracking software allow you to monitor traffic sources, track conversions, and identify high-performing content and campaigns. By leveraging data-driven insights, you can refine your strategies, optimize conversions, and allocate resources more effectively.

2. SEO and Keyword Research Tools:

Search engine optimization (SEO) plays a crucial role in driving organic traffic to your affiliate site or content. Tools such as SEMrush, Ahrefs, or Moz enable you to conduct comprehensive keyword research, analyze competitor strategies, and optimize your content for relevant search queries. By identifying high-volume keywords with low competition, you can enhance your site's visibility in search engine results pages (SERPs), attract targeted traffic, and increase your affiliate revenue.

Chapter 16: Your Affiliate Marketing Tool Box

3. Content Management Systems (CMS):

A robust CMS is essential for creating, managing, and optimizing content across your affiliate marketing channels. Popular platforms like WordPress, Drupal, or Joomla provide user-friendly interfaces, customizable templates, and plugins/extensions that streamline content creation and publication. With a CMS, you can publish SEO-optimized blog posts, landing pages, product reviews, and multimedia content to engage your audience and drive conversions effectively.

4. Email Marketing Automation Tools:

Email marketing remains a potent tool for nurturing leads, building relationships with your audience, and promoting affiliate products or services. Platforms

Chapter 16: Your Affiliate Marketing Tool Box

like Mailchimp, ConvertKit, or HubSpot offer automation features that enable you to create personalized email campaigns, segment your audience based on behavior or demographics, and track campaign performance metrics (e.g., open rates, click-through rates). By delivering targeted, relevant content to subscribers, you can drive conversions and maximize affiliate commissions.

5. Social Media Management and Analytics

Social media platforms are invaluable channels for promoting affiliate products, engaging with your audience, and driving traffic to your affiliate links. Tools such as Buffer, Hootsuite, or Sprout Social facilitate social media management by scheduling posts, monitoring mentions, and analyzing performance metrics (e.g., engagement

Chapter 16: Your Affiliate Marketing Tool Box

rates, follower growth). Leveraging social media analytics helps you understand audience preferences, optimize content strategies, and capitalize on trends to maximize reach and engagement.

6. Affiliate Networks and Platforms:

Affiliate networks and platforms serve as intermediaries between affiliates (publishers) and merchants (advertisers), facilitating affiliate program management, commission tracking, and payment processing. Popular networks like Amazon Associates, ShareASale, or CJ Affiliate (formerly Commission Junction) offer access to a diverse range of affiliate programs across various industries. By joining reputable networks, you gain access to a broader selection of products/services to promote, competitive commission rates,

Chapter 16: Your Affiliate Marketing Tool Box

and robust reporting tools for monitoring performance.

7. Conversion Rate Optimization (CRO) Tools:

CRO tools are instrumental in optimizing your affiliate marketing campaigns to maximize conversions and revenue generation. Tools such as Optimizely, Unbounce, or Google Optimize enable you to conduct A/B testing, create responsive landing pages, and analyze user behavior through heatmaps and click-tracking tools. By experimenting with different design elements, calls-to-action (CTAs), and conversion funnels, you can identify and

Chapter 17: The Future of Affiliate Marketing

Chapter 17:
The Future of Affiliate Marketing:

Affiliate marketing has evolved significantly since its inception, driven by technological advancements, changing consumer behaviors, and industry innovations. As we look ahead, the future of affiliate marketing promises to be dynamic, transformative, and ripe with opportunities for growth and adaptation.

Embracing AI and Machine Learning:

One of the most profound shifts in affiliate marketing is the integration of artificial intelligence (AI) and machine learning (ML) technologies. These advancements enable marketers to leverage predictive analytics,

Chapter 17: The Future of Affiliate Marketing

personalized recommendations, and automated content creation to enhance targeting precision and optimize customer experiences. AI-driven algorithms can analyze vast amounts of data in real-time, allowing affiliates to tailor their strategies based on individual preferences, behaviors, and purchasing patterns.

Rise of Influencer Partnerships:

Influencer marketing continues to reshape the affiliate landscape, with social media influencers wielding significant influence over consumer purchasing decisions. Collaborating with influencers allows affiliates to tap into niche audiences, build authenticity, and drive engagement through genuine endorsements and storytelling. As brands seek more authentic connections

Chapter 17: The Future of Affiliate Marketing

with consumers, influencer partnerships are poised to become integral to affiliate marketing strategies, offering brands unparalleled reach and credibility.

Mobile-First Strategies:

The proliferation of mobile devices has transformed how consumers interact with content and make purchasing decisions. Mobile-first affiliate strategies emphasize responsive design, fast-loading websites, and intuitive user experiences tailored for smartphones and tablets. With mobile commerce (m-commerce) on the rise, affiliates must prioritize mobile optimization to capitalize on impulsive buying behaviors and ensure seamless transactions across devices.

Chapter 17: The Future of Affiliate Marketing

Content Diversification and Personalization:

Content remains the cornerstone of successful affiliate marketing campaigns, but its evolution toward diversification and personalization is crucial. Beyond traditional blog posts and reviews, affiliates are embracing multimedia formats such as video tutorials, podcasts, and interactive content to engage audiences and drive conversions. Personalized content strategies leverage data insights to deliver targeted messaging, product recommendations, and offers tailored to individual preferences, enhancing relevance and fostering deeper connections with consumers.

Chapter 17: The Future of Affiliate Marketing

Blockchain and Transparency:

Blockchain technology is poised to revolutionize affiliate marketing by enhancing transparency, combating fraud, and improving transactional security. Decentralized affiliate networks powered by blockchain enable direct peer-to-peer interactions, smart contract automation, and immutable tracking of affiliate commissions and performance metrics. This decentralized approach fosters trust among affiliates, merchants, and consumers by ensuring transparency in payment processes and eliminating intermediaries.

Chapter 17: The Future of Affiliate Marketing

Regulatory Compliance and Ethical Practices:

As the affiliate marketing industry matures, regulatory scrutiny and consumer demand for ethical practices continue to shape its future. Affiliates must adhere to data protection regulations (e.g., GDPR, CCPA) and ethical guidelines to safeguard consumer privacy and maintain trust. Transparent disclosure of affiliate relationships, honest product reviews, and compliance with advertising standards are essential to fostering long-term credibility and sustainability in the evolving affiliate landscape.

Chapter 17: The Future of Affiliate Marketing

Sustainability and Corporate Responsibility:

Increasingly, consumers are prioritizing sustainability and corporate responsibility when making purchasing decisions. Affiliates can align with eco-friendly brands, promote sustainable products, and advocate for social causes to resonate with conscientious consumers. Embracing sustainable practices not only enhances brand reputation but also attracts environmentally conscious audiences who value ethical consumption and support brands committed to positive social impact.

Chapter 17: The Future of Affiliate Marketing

Continuous Adaptation and Innovation:

The future of affiliate marketing hinges on continuous adaptation to emerging trends, consumer preferences, and technological advancements. Affiliates must embrace agility, experimentation, and innovation to stay ahead of the curve and capitalize on evolving opportunities. Whether through AI-driven automation, influencer collaborations, mobile optimization, or blockchain integration, proactive adaptation to industry shifts ensures sustained relevance and competitiveness in the dynamic affiliate marketing ecosystem.

Chapter 17: The Future of Affiliate Marketing

As affiliate marketing evolves, embracing technological innovation, consumer-centric strategies, and ethical principles will be paramount to long-term success. By harnessing the power of AI, cultivating authentic influencer partnerships, prioritizing mobile experiences, and championing transparency and sustainability, affiliates can navigate the future landscape with confidence. The future promises unprecedented possibilities for growth, creativity, and impact in affiliate marketing, inviting affiliates to embrace change and pioneer new paths toward continued success.

Chapter 18: Why I Struggled to be Successful with Affiliate Marketing

Chapter 18:
Why I Struggled to be Successful with Affiliate Marketing

Affiliate marketing, with its promise of passive income and flexible work hours, lures many aspiring entrepreneurs into its fold. Yet, behind the allure lies a landscape fraught with challenges and complexities that can lead even the most enthusiastic marketer to stumble. Reflecting on my own journey, I've come to understand the multifaceted reasons why many, including myself, face hurdles in this competitive arena.

Chapter 18: Why I Struggled to be Successful with Affiliate Marketing

Misunderstanding the Scope of Affiliate Marketing:

One of the initial pitfalls in affiliate marketing is underestimating the breadth and depth of what it entails. It's not just about slapping affiliate links onto a website or social media profile; it's about understanding consumer psychology, mastering SEO techniques, creating compelling content, and continuously optimizing strategies to stay relevant in a dynamic market. The misconception that affiliate marketing is a quick path to riches overlooks the strategic planning and persistent effort required for sustainable success.

Chapter 18: Why I Struggled to be Successful with Affiliate Marketing

Failing to Build a Strong Foundation:

Success in affiliate marketing hinges on a solid foundation built on market research, niche selection, and audience targeting. Without a clear understanding of your target audience's needs, pain points, and purchasing behaviors, efforts to promote affiliate products can miss the mark. Building credibility and trust with your audience takes time and consistent effort, and neglecting this foundational step can lead to disengagement and lackluster results.

Lack of Consistent and Strategic Content Creation:

Content is the lifeblood of affiliate marketing, serving as the bridge between potential customers and

Chapter 18: Why I Struggled to be Successful with Affiliate Marketing

affiliate products. However, inconsistent or haphazard content creation can undermine your credibility and hinder audience engagement. Successful affiliates strategically plan their content to address audience interests, solve problems, and provide value consistently over time. Without a cohesive content strategy aligned with audience expectations, maintaining relevance and driving conversions becomes challenging.

Over Reliance on Passive Income Expectations:

One of the allurements of affiliate marketing is its promise of passive income—a revenue stream that continues to generate earnings with minimal ongoing effort. However, achieving sustainable passive income

Chapter 18: Why I Struggled to be Successful with Affiliate Marketing

requires significant upfront investment in time, effort, and resources to build and scale your affiliate business. Many newcomers to affiliate marketing underestimate the initial workload and overestimate the speed at which passive income streams will materialize, leading to frustration and disillusionment when results don't align with expectations.

Inadequate Traffic Generation and Conversion Optimization:

Driving traffic to your affiliate links and converting visitors into customers are fundamental challenges in affiliate marketing. Effective SEO strategies, social media engagement, email marketing campaigns, and paid advertising are essential tools for attracting targeted traffic. However,

Chapter 18: Why I Struggled to be Successful with Affiliate Marketing

without a nuanced understanding of these channels and how they intersect with your audience's purchasing journey, efforts to generate traffic can fall short. Similarly, optimizing conversion rates requires continuous testing, refinement of landing pages, and understanding of consumer behavior—areas where novice affiliates may struggle initially.

Neglecting Relationship Building and Networking:

Successful affiliate marketing often hinges on forging meaningful relationships with industry peers, influencers, and stakeholders. Collaborations, partnerships, and networking can amplify your reach, credibility, and opportunities for growth. However, neglecting to invest in relationship building and networking can

Chapter 18: Why I Struggled to be Successful with Affiliate Marketing

limit your visibility within the affiliate community and hinder access to valuable resources, mentorship, and collaborative opportunities.

Lack of Resilience and Adaptability:

The affiliate marketing landscape is dynamic, characterized by evolving consumer trends, algorithm updates, and competitive shifts. Adapting to these changes requires resilience, flexibility, and a willingness to pivot strategies based on market conditions and performance metrics. Many individuals falter when faced with setbacks or unforeseen challenges, lacking the perseverance and adaptability needed to navigate the inherent uncertainties of affiliate marketing.

Chapter 18: Why I Struggled to be Successful with Affiliate Marketing

Conclusion: Lessons Learned and Moving Forward

My journey in affiliate marketing has been marked by both successes and failures, each offering valuable lessons for growth and refinement. Recognizing the complexities and challenges—whether in understanding market dynamics, building a robust foundation, or maintaining resilience—has illuminated pathways to overcoming obstacles and achieving sustainable success. Aspiring affiliates must approach the journey with realistic expectations, strategic foresight, and a commitment to continuous learning and adaptation. By addressing these multifaceted challenges head-on, aspiring affiliates can forge a resilient

Chapter 18: Why I Struggled to be Successful with Affiliate Marketing

path forward in the dynamic world of affiliate marketing.

Chapter 19: Conclusion...Your Journey Begins Now!

Chapter 19: Conclusion...Your Journey Begins Now!

As you near the end of this journey into the world of affiliate marketing, it's essential to reflect on what you've learned and consider your next steps thoughtfully. Affiliate marketing offers a pathway to financial independence and entrepreneurial freedom, but success requires dedication, strategic planning, and a willingness to navigate both highs and lows along the way.

Before embarking on your affiliate marketing journey, take time to assess if this path aligns with your goals, skills, and ambitions. Are you passionate about a particular niche or industry? Do you have the discipline to consistently create valuable content and engage with your audience? Are you prepared for the

Chapter 19: Conclusion...Your Journey Begins Now!

initial investment of time and resources required to build a sustainable affiliate business? Honest self-assessment will clarify if affiliate marketing is a viable fit for your aspirations and lifestyle.

In the early stages of your affiliate marketing venture, financial expectations should be grounded in realistic projections. While affiliate marketing can yield passive income over time, initial investments in website hosting, content creation tools, marketing expenses, and potentially paid advertising campaigns are common. Budgeting for these expenses and understanding that returns may be gradual can mitigate financial stress and position you for long-term success.

Chapter 19: Conclusion...Your Journey Begins Now!

As you finish reading this book...think about these **next steps**:

1. Refine Your Niche Strategy:
Based on your interests and market research, refine your niche strategy to target a specific audience effectively. Focus on creating high-quality content that addresses audience needs and aligns with affiliate product offerings.

2. Build and Optimize Your Platform:
Invest in building a user-friendly website or blog that serves as your affiliate marketing hub. Optimize your platform for SEO, ensuring that your content ranks well in search engines and attracts organic traffic.

3. Develop Content Strategy:
Create a comprehensive content strategy that includes regular blog posts, videos, podcasts, or social media

Chapter 19: Conclusion…Your Journey Begins Now!

content. Prioritize quality over quantity, aiming to educate, inspire, and engage your audience while subtly integrating affiliate links.

4. Network and Collaborate:

 Forge relationships with industry peers, influencers, and potential affiliate partners. Collaborations and partnerships can expand your reach, enhance credibility, and open doors to new opportunities within the affiliate marketing ecosystem.

5. Monitor and Adapt:

Continuously monitor key performance indicators (KPIs) such as traffic, conversion rates, and affiliate earnings. Analyze data insights to refine your strategies, experiment with new approaches, and adapt to changing market dynamics.

Chapter 19: Conclusion...Your Journey Begins Now!

Finally, as you embark on your affiliate marketing journey, embrace the learning experiences, challenges, and triumphs that await. Remember, success in affiliate marketing is not solely defined by monetary gains but also by the impact you make on your audience and the relationships you cultivate within your niche. Stay resilient in the face of setbacks, remain adaptable to industry shifts, and continue to innovate and grow as an affiliate marketer.

Chapter 19: Conclusion…Your Journey Begins Now!

A Final Word from the Failurenaire:

Dear Reader,

As we conclude this journey together, I want to commend you for your commitment and enthusiasm in exploring the world of affiliate marketing. Whether you're just starting or seeking to refine your strategies, remember that every step forward is a step towards realizing your entrepreneurial dreams.

Affiliate marketing, like any venture, has its challenges, but it also holds boundless opportunities for creativity, growth, and personal fulfillment. Trust in your abilities, stay focused on your goals, and let your passion for your niche guide you through the ups and downs of this dynamic industry.

Chapter 19: Conclusion...Your Journey Begins Now!

May this book serve as a compass on your path to affiliate marketing success, providing insights, strategies, and inspiration to fuel your journey. Embrace the power of persistence, innovation, and authenticity as you carve your unique niche in the affiliate marketing landscape. Remember, this book is supposed to be used for entertainment purposes only. Most people will NOT have success with Affiliate Marketing but it can be done! If this side hustle does not seem like the one for you...be sure to check out some of my other Side Hustle Series books.

Thank you for joining me on this transformative adventure. Here's to your success as an affiliate marketer!

Warm regards,

The Failurenaire

www.ingramcontent.com/pod-product-compliance
Lightning Source LLC
Chambersburg PA
CBHW071929210526
45479CB00002B/605